ASTROLOG COMPLETE GUIDES

OMENS and SUPERSTITIONS

Sara Zed

Astrolog Publishing House

Astrolog Publishing House

P. O. Box 1123, Hod Hasharon 45111, Israel

Tel: 972-9-7412044

Fax: 972-9-7442714

E-Mail: info@astrolog.co.il

Astrolog Web Site: www.astrolog.co.il

© 2002 Astrolog Publishing House

ISBN 965-494-146-5

Published by Astrolog Publishing House 2002

10 9 8 7 6 5 4 3 2 1

Superstitions? What, How, and Why... 7

Superstitions? what, how, and why...

A superstition can be defined in various ways by distinguishing between two main approaches: the first is defining the superstition through the person's eyes; the second is defining it by understanding it.

In any case, we are speaking about an idea to which we attribute properties of actualization. This idea can occur in the form of a thought, or in the form of an object that is linked to a thought, or in the form of a ceremony, a prayer, and so on. Sometimes, a superstition is linked to some kind of omen that foretells the future. Whatever it is, it is important to remember that a superstition is an idea, an expression of thought, that the person believes can be expressed in the material world.

A superstition depends first and foremost on the person's cultural background - for instance, in every religion, there are many customs that are considered to be superstitions by secular people. For a sworn atheist, every religious ceremony is superstition for its own sake. In Christianity, for instance, there is a clear differentiation between "true religious belief" (religio) and a "false" superstition (superstitio).

The origin of many superstitions lies in religion or ancient magic, and remnants of the ancient belief reach us either as religious procedures or as ostensibly inexplicable beliefs. When the members of a Native American tribe dance under the heavens in order to bring rain, is it superstition or religion? Or when people say the prayer for rain, or draw a circle and remain inside it, as the Wiccans do, is it religion or superstition?

Regarding every custom and belief, we have to examine the background from which the believer himself comes. Kissing the mezuzah is a Jewish custom, but there is no doubt that a Christian would view this custom as a superstition; eating the sacramental wafer is a Christian custom - but a Jew would perceive it as a superstition.

Sometimes, the same belief, the same custom, has different - and occasionally opposite - meanings in different cultures: the number 13 can be an unlucky number in one culture and a lucky one in another!

It is important to remember that a superstition is first and foremost an attempt to make the unreal real, to attribute properties of "matter" to an idea that is "spirit."

Let's take the example of walking under a ladder leaning against a wall. The idea that such an action brings bad luck belongs to the spiritual realm, but if we perform the action - the physical passage, the result will be bad luck that is expressed physically.

Even when the superstition relates to a tangible, material element - such as an amulet or a physical sign - or to a particular ceremony, the superstition is more important than the object itself. A horseshoe influences us greatly - not because it's a horseshoe, but because we believe that it has an influence!

Many people compare the superstition to a "mental reflex" action that is imprinted into the person's heritage.

In order to understand this, let's imagine a situation where a person suddenly finds a heavy sword pointing at him. His first reaction is to draw back, to blink, to flex his muscles, and so on. This is a very reasonable physical response.

When the same person is sitting in a safe and comfortable seat in a movie theater, and the same sword points at him from the screen, his physical reactions are identical to those in the first case, except that he knows for sure that he is in no real physical danger!

Why?

Because a subconscious physical reflex is at work in him - a mysterious system that turns the "make-believe" situation into reality. Or, in other words, the person's life experience - the collective human experience, the human culture - imprints a reflex or instinct in him, instructing him to react in a physical manner to a threat - even to a "make-believe" threat.

Many researchers claim that the superstition is exactly the same reflex or instinct in the person's mental realm. When a person sees a black cat crossing his path, he operates according to a "mental reflex" even though his logic is telling him clearly that he is not in any danger.

There are mental, instinctive reflexes imprinted in every person - according to his culture, his heritage, his experience in life - that affect him. These reflexes are activated by a "mental trigger" - exactly in the same way as the drawn sword is a "physical trigger" that "pushes" and activates the reflex.

These triggers, some of which are common to an entire culture and some of which are unique to each person, are superstitions.

These superstitions are stronger than any scientific logic, and they are detached from the person's "cultural level," education, or "approach" to life. They exist independently, sometimes buried for many years in the depths of the person's soul and spirit, and then they come up to the surface at the most surprising moments!

Superstitions are inextricably linked to the prediction of the future. This is when we talk about omens, not superstitions, but they are more alike than they are different. A superstition works, according to those who believe in it, on the person's luck or future fate. It is an omen of what will happen in the future.

For this reason, we must be aware of the difference between a superstition and an omen. In both cases, it is a question of the future, of change - but in the case of a superstition, the change is through fate or luck - for good or for bad.

Omens that indicate the future - such as "a flock of birds in the sky predicts rain," "fleeing rats indicate an imminent shipwreck," and so on - are generally layers of cumulative human experience. In ancient times, man lived "inside" nature, saw phenomena that recurred in a fixed, cyclical manner, and drew conclusions regarding omens of the future.

However, how can we explain that "a virgin who sits at the corner of the table will not marry for seven years"? Is this an omen or a superstition?

Superstitions - and here we include omens as well - are ideas with deep roots in human culture, and the belief in them is without any real logical basis. Superstitions are first and foremost beliefs - that is, they exist, for anyone who believes in them, and he does not doubt them despite their "lack of logic."

In fact, superstition exists in everyone's heart to some extent. Even people who consider themselves free of any superstition display a "mental reflex" in response to one or another belief during their lives - birth, death, marriage or divorce, for instance.

When superstitions are collected for research, this must be done "in depth and in breadth." On the one hand, we must go back to the roots of human culture, and try as get as close as possible to the primal origin of the belief itself. For this reason, we must get to various sources - most of them religious or magic, but also in the field of art, literature or material culture - in order to know "how the belief grew."

On the other hand, we must investigate the various cultures in breadth, in order to see how a particular belief is expressed - identically or differently - in them.

The total number of superstitions in the world has been estimated by researchers to be between 120,000 and a quarter of a million.

It is obvious that research or a book that deals with this topic presents only the "cream," the most common and most notable superstitions that have the greatest significance (and generally speaking, these are also the most interesting or "juicy" ones). I'm sure that however many superstitions we present, there will always be some that were overlooked.

A recent study that was conducted on several hundred adults examined the spread of superstitions. The subjects were asked to mention the superstitions they had encountered (not necessarily ones in which they believed). Each subject was asked to mention only five superstitions.

It transpired that in total, over 600 superstitions were mentioned - in other words, almost every subject had his own "private" superstition. This attests to the tremendous variety in this field. However, on the other hand, it turned out that the "leading" superstitions were given a substantial number of votes - that is, there was a broad consensus concerning "accepted" superstitions.

The list of the ten superstitions that received the highest number of votes is as follows:
1. A black cat
2. A wishbone

3. Walking under a ladder
4. A horseshoe
5. Spilled salt
6. Starting something on the left foot
7. A rabbit's foot
8. The number 7
9. A shooting star
10. A broken mirror

And by the way, four researchers participated in the study - all of them experts in the field of superstitions. All four of them were asked to prepare a parallel list (before the actual study) in which they had to guess the first ten superstitions, not in any particular order. Two of the researchers guessed four items, the third guessed five, and the fourth guessed seven of the items in the list.

A similar study, which was conducted in Britain, produced the following list:
1. A wishbone
2. A horseshoe
3. A rabbit's foot
4. A four-leafed clover
5. A broken mirror
6. Getting up on the wrong side of the bed
7. Walking under a ladder
8. Friday the 13th
9. Spilling salt
10. A shooting star

We can immediately see that in superstitions, despite the influence of the heritage, there is a great deal of similarity between the different cultures.

Abracadabra

This is a magic word that serves as a protective charm when it is thought or pronounced aloud. Other superstitions attribute to the word the power to cure diseases and infections, as well as the power to grant sleep and bring the beloved to the lover. The sound of the word is identical in many languages.

When the word is written in the shape of a pyramid, it serves as a charm in itself. It is usually written on parchment inside a piece of jewelry that hangs round the neck on a chain.

When a person is ill, he must draw this pyramid several times, each time erasing a letter, and the disease will fade away. Similarly, a person who wants to strengthen his beloved's love for him, for instance, inscribes the pyramid starting from the letter "A", and in this way, love will become stronger with every additional letter.

Magic words are common in human culture. The abracadabra pyramid apparently originates from the Jewish Kabbala, even though it first appears in the writings of Septimus Severus, a Roman physician of the second century AD. According to the Kabbala sages, it was used as an amulet against the evil eye (although the expression is in fact the Christian trinity of father, son, and holy ghost). Another possible origin of the word is the Jewish concept of "I will bless the Creator" (avarech et haboreh), which was later altered in Christianity.

In the olden days, it was believed that the word itself - the very mention of the word verbally, in writing, or in thought - had a great deal of magic power. The explicit name of God in Judaism has a tremendous effect on both speaker and hearer. Over the last generations, the word "abracadabra" passed from the realm of magic more into that of enchantments and hypnosis.

Daniel Defoe, the well-known author of *Robinson Crusoe*, writes in his book, *A Journal of the Plague Year* (1722) that the most effective way of stopping the plague is by writing the magic word on parchment, burning the parchment, and mixing the ashes with water, which served as purifying water.

Occasionally the amulet appears in a rhomboid shape - that is, the amulet starts from the letter "A," adding a letter until it reaches the entire word, and then goes back to the letter "A."

It must be noted that the importance of the word does not lie in its linguistic meaning, but rather mainly in its strange sound. From this point of view, it is linguistically similar to "hocus pocus."

abracadabra
abracadabr
abracadab
abracada
abracad
abraca
abrac
abra
abr
ab
a

Acorn

The acorn, the fruit of the oak tree, is very important as an amulet. The origin of this belief lies in the Druid culture, which believed that the acorn brought good luck to the person who carried it, and it is obvious that this is linked to the acorn being the seed of the sacred oak tree. This superstition is prevalent in the Mediterranean countries, where the oak is widespread. The acorn links man with nature and protects him from the evil spirits of nature.

A custom that has survived to this day is to place an acorn or a string of acorns, on the windowsill. Some people grind a dried acorn and sprinkle the powder in the house, mainly to protect the house and its occupants from fire or lightning.

The acorn is a seed that takes a very long time to sprout, so it is a good idea for a person who has difficulties on the way to realizing his ambitions to take an acorn as an amulet. In this way, he will gain the perseverance, patience, and tolerance of the acorn.

Acting

There are many superstitions linked to acting, theater, and actors, and sometimes it seems impossible to track actors' customs and conversations without using a database of superstitions. The problem becomes even more complicated because many actors have their "private" superstitions in addition to the general ones.

No self-respecting actor will use dressing room number 13, or a dressing room in which a picture of a person is hanging. After the dressing room has been selected, he must ensure that the mirror is not located opposite the door; superstition has it that if anyone sees the face of the actor reflected in the mirror while he is putting on his make-up, the play is bound to be a flop.

There must always be a rabbit's foot on the dressing table, especially in cases of some item of make-up falling to the ground, which is a very bad sign indeed. In contrast, the custom of pouring white talc or any other white powder on the dressing-room floor before leaving the room is widespread. It is good to step on the powder before leaving the room. A wig brings good luck to the actor, so actors are in the habit of keeping a lot of wigs in their dressing rooms, whether they are necessary or not.

In order to know whether a show will succeed or fail - and this is especially true of actresses - the actor must stand on the threshold of the dressing room before the première of the play and kick both shoes off into the room. If both shoes land on their soles, the play will be an incredible success. But the actor must be careful while kicking, because if his shoes hit the mirror and crack it, it would be better to cancel the show before the curtain goes up for the first time!

The actor must leave the dressing room left foot first, and he must go on stage right foot first.

If an actor falls onstage, he will act in many plays on the stage (and that is the origin of the actors' "blessing" - "Break a leg!").

Peacock feathers bring bad luck, as do ostrich feathers. Artificial flowers are preferable to fresh flowers, both on and off stage. And the words "Good luck!" must never be uttered before the curtain goes up.

The night before the première, an actor must sleep with a script of the play under his pillow, otherwise he will forget his lines.

An actor or actress who has to change costumes during the play must turn around on his or her heels in a clockwise direction after taking off the old costume and before putting on the new one.

And of course, if you hate the director, the playwright, or one of the actors, all you have to do is go across stage or backstage whistling loudly - and this will serve as the final straw that causes the show to be a total flop.

Amulet

Amulets, in general, are objects whose purpose is to stop evil and promote good. The amulet must be kept within the field of action of good or evil, since its range of operation is limited. (For this reason, an amulet is carried on the person, or is placed at the entrance to the house, and so on.)

There is a difference between a "natural" amulet and a man-made one. A natural amulet is in fact an everyday object that, in addition to its regular use, is also used as an amulet - a horseshoe, for instance. Sometimes it is part of a whole body or object, such as a rabbit's foot or a rhinoceros horn, and so on.

A man-made amulet is an object that is manufactured to serve specifically as an amulet. It can be a cross for Christians, a mezuzah for Jews, a hamsa (hand) for Moslems, or an image of Buddha for Buddhists - this is an amulet that we define as man-made.

There are amulets that combine sound and form, such as a bell that hangs at the entrance to a house, or a whistle on the roof through which the wind whistles. Other amulets make use of certain odors - usually perfumes.

Color is extremely important, as is the material from which the amulet is made. A horseshoe must be made of iron, but a bell made of gold will be "stronger" than one made of iron.

There are many amulets that come from the plant or animal world - red pepper, for instance, is a very common amulet against the evil eye. Various birds and fish are good luck amulets.

Many superstitions are linked to amulets, and the number of amulets in the various cultures is as large as the number of superstitions.

Ankh

The ankh is a special symbol, somewhat similar to a cross, which originated in the hieroglyphics of ancient Egypt. The meaning of the concept is "life." In etchings and paintings, we can see that the pharaohs are holding this symbol in their hands. In Egyptian literature, the symbol is also called "the key of life."

Today, the ankh is considered to be a sign with unique power, not particularly as an omen of life, but more in the sexual realm. (The sign of the ankh is in fact the basis of the symbol of Venus in astrology). The symbol is supposed to reinforce the person's sexuality, and many people have an ankh tattooed next to or on their genitals.

In Greece, the sign had a slightly different meaning. It is similar to the letter **T**, which indicates life, and when it is inverted, it signifies eternity. That is, eternal life.

Today, the ankh appears in jewelry and numerous ornaments, especially jewelry worn around the neck.

Ants

A widespread superstition has it that when you step on an ants' nest, it is a sign of heavy rain. This superstition has backing in many countries in which rain falls after a heatwave. The heat causes the ants to go up to the surface in order to open "air holes."

An ants' nest opposite the entrance to the house is a promise of happiness and wealth.

Ants do not need sleep, according to the superstition, and the person who wants to turn his nights into days should sit on an ants' nest, because this is a remedy against sleep.

Ants' eggs are used - usually with honey - as a love potion and as a means of increasing virility.

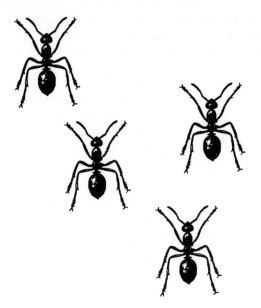

Apple

Before eating an apple, it must be wiped very, very well on one's lapel in order to get rid of the devil!

If a woman has cheated on her husband, her apple pie will go sour by evening.

An apple a day keeps the doctor away!

The apple has a great deal of significance in superstition, especially in everything concerning women's health and romantic feelings. An apple that changes in color from green to red, and at the same time turns from sour to sweet, contributed a great deal about the apple's influence to superstitions. For instance, the apple is a means of finding true love.

A woman can write the letters of the alphabet on the skin of a ripe apple and then peel it. She must try to peel it in one unbroken strip, but in the place where the peel breaks off, she will find the first letter of her intended lover's name.

Another way is to peel the apple in as long a strip as possible, write the letters of the alphabet in order on it, and throw the peel over one's right shoulder. The place where the peel tears indicates the first letter of the beloved's name.

Because of its health value, the apple was considered to be the fruit of the gods that grants eternal youth, and that is why the gods keep their apple orchard behind a high wall and under lock and key. To a certain extent, this goes back to the story of the Garden of Eden - the fruit that opened Adam and Eve's eyes, according to popular tradition, was an apple. As a result, the apple - especially a ripe, red apple - is considered to be a fruit of sexual temptation in addition to being an "eye-opener."

In many places, if a woman offers a man a red apple, it is a clear sign of her intention to seduce him.

In Latin countries, a married woman is forbidden to give an apple to a man who is not her husband.

In various cultures - Jewish, European, or Islamic - the apple is a "drug of life" and is used in natural medicine. Its healing properties are also manifested in the fact that in many legends we find a golden apple as a central symbol.

The interesting thing in all the cultures is that there is a link between the apple and a stable family life. "He who does not marry a woman will have a cold apple pie on his table."

April 1st

This date, April Fool's Day in many traditions, is a particular day in the year with special customs. For instance, there are people who believe that a lie "doesn't count" on this day, so it is permissible to lie, or to play tricks on others on April 1st.

April 1st symbolizes the beginning of the summer - but between that date and the summer the weather is still unclear and unstable.

April 1st is also considered by many as "a day that doesn't exist," so everything is permitted. This belief derives from the changes and adjustments in the Gregorian calendar in 1752. (A solar year is 365 days plus a little, and despite the adjustments of the month of February, it is necessary to make a "large" adjustment in the calendar every few hundred years.)

Axe

The axe has certain magical properties, mainly in communities where the earth is worked. When cattle or horses step over an axe that is lying in the entrance to the pen, their health improves, and if they are stolen, they will return to their owners by themselves. But a much more important superstition prohibits carrying an axe within the walls of the house - because this is an omen of imminent death! The axe must be left outside in the yard, preferably stuck in a tree trunk.

(In many countries, the axe is considered to be the tool of the gravedigger; for this reason, its place is not inside the house.)

Bad news thrown to the wind

When a person has to be the bearer of bad news, especially concerning a recent death, it is better for him first to break the news "to the wind." The origin of this superstition lies in the custom of blaming the bearer of ill tidings for the bad news. When the bearer announces the news to the "wind," the wind becomes the one that bears the bad tidings to the other people.

There are different forms of this superstition: In Europe, for instance, a person who has to break the news of a death looks for a beehive or ants' nest, and tells them the bad news. A flock of birds is also suitable for this purpose. In South America, it is customary to go up to a high cliff and shout the news into the wind. In India, the news is delivered to the flowing waters of a river. In many places in the world, it is customary for the bearer of bad news to shout it from inside a thicket of bushes or trees.

In all of these cases, this belief provides protection for the bearer of ill tidings, and if he employs one of these methods, he will not be blamed for the bad news, and his head will remain firmly on his shoulders!

Baldness

There are many superstitions linked to baldness, and one of them is that baldness begins when a person has a haircut on a night with a full moon. The hair falls out, and ultimately the bald pate appears! There is no doubt that the source of the belief lies in the similarity between a bald pate and a full moon.

In order to prevent balding, the most widespread popular remedy is goose fat, which must be rubbed into the scalp daily.

A common superstition is that people with bald pates must not be trusted, and that is one of the reasons why men wear hats. It is also the origin of the custom of removing the hat every time it is necessary to express innocence and integrity.

And of course, there is the opinion that men with bald pates are very virile, and are more potent than men with luxuriant heads of hair - the only problem being that they don't have too many opportunities to prove it!

Bat

The bat has always been linked to the devil, to witches, and to the forces of darkness and evil. Because of the peculiar manner in which the bat sleeps - hanging upside down - the superstition states that the devil or his henchmen sleep in the form of a bat when they rest. Since the bat is active at night, like the forces of darkness, this suits the devil's schedule. In other sources, the bat appears as the devil's assistant, like the wolf or the cat.

Another superstition says that the bat takes the souls of the dead, so a home or place where there are bats attests to restless ghosts that are wondering about.

Walter Scott, the author, wrote to his friend: "If you see a bat going up and coming back to the ground, know that the bewitching hour is approaching, the hour when the creatures of darkness take over people's souls."

The blood and body parts of bats were considered to contain great magical power. The fact that the bat is a warm-blooded mammal in the form of a bird is the reason for this. There is almost no witches' potion that does not contain something of the bat.

An additional superstition says that the bat grabs hold of a woman's hair when something is bothering her conscience, and tries to drag her to the witch or the devil - and perhaps that is the source of the deep fear of bats!

There are cultures in which the bat is a positive omen. In China and India, the bat is considered to be a very intelligent creature, similar to the owl. That is why it flies with its head inclined downward (because of the weight of its head). In China, the bat is considered an omen of long life, and it brings good luck to the home in which it resides.

In England, Ireland, and Scotland, the bat is a symbol

of death, "A bat in the house is a sign of another grave to be dug at nightfall!"

Powder from dried bat (some people say dried bat's heart) will prevent the soldier from being wounded in battle, and will staunch a wounded man's bleeding during battle.

A person who washes his eyes and face in bat's blood will see like a cat at night!

When a bat enters the room, or grasps a person's hair, only the sound of thunder and the light of lightning can drive it away!

Witches use bat's blood in order to be able to fly. Similarly, bat's blood is used as a love potion, as well as for curing sick horses.

In Scandinavian countries, a dried bat worn on the body is an extremely valuable amulet of continuing love. In the United States, a dried bat's heart is a very valuable amulet for gamblers. (Gambling, in any case, is the devil's playground.)

In the southern United States, a person who is pursued by a ghost must find a hair of a black cat, throw it over his left shoulder, and spit three times. The ghost will turn into a bat and disappear into the darkness.

In Africa, bats are considered to be the remnants of the souls of the dead, so a bat hovering over a house is "waiting" for another soul.

In other places, the bat is thought to guard against the damage caused by extreme weather.

Beard

Beware of a person whose hair is one color, and whose beard is another!

A man with a red beard has a temperament saturated with blood.

A woman with a beard is not to be trusted - nor is a man without one!

The beard has always been an important part of a man's life, and there are many superstitions linked to it. When Alexander of Macedonia fought the Persian army, he noticed that the Persian warriors sported black beards, and the longer the beard, the higher the rank.

In response, Alexander ordered his warriors to shave off their beards so that they would not get in the way during battle, and so that the older and more experienced warriors could not be identified. This is the origin of the belief that a warrior who shaves before battle will be victorious.

The beard is generally linked to wisdom, masculinity, and maturity - young boys and eunuchs are beardless. Another important link concerning wisdom is with religion. In most cultures, religious functionaries are bearded. The fact that the beard grows daily, and its growth can actually be seen, even after shaving, symbolizes the eternal cyclical nature of creation. "The day the sun doesn't shine and the beard doesn't grow will mark the end of the foundations of the earth!"

The hair of the beard, similar to the nails or the eyelashes, is part of the person's body, and when it falls into the hands of someone with evil intentions, it can be used against him. It is dangerous to trim the beard or shave in a place where the devil may be - since he is liable to pick up the hair and then gain control of the person's soul. For this reason, the hair trimmings are burned, and the whiskers are flushed away.

To this day, the Muslims are in the habit of swearing "on Mohammed's beard." Among religious Jews, the beard is sacred. In ancient Greece, the terms "wise man" or "bearded man" are identical in linguistic structure.

The beard is also the symbol of the king. When a beardless youth accedes to the throne, or a princess (as in ancient Egypt), a golden beard is placed on his/her chin, and that is how he/she appears in public. In ancient Egypt, an artisan who created a statue or relief of a Pharaoh, prince, or princess without a beard was put to death!

In Babylon, Persia, and Egypt, it was customary to groom the beard, comb it, and anoint it with perfume - something which was done to the hair on the head only much later.

While a man's beard is a symbol of standing, a woman's beard links her to the forces of darkness! A woman with a beard was considered to be a messenger of the witch on earth, and was liable to be burned at the stake during the Middle Ages.

Maybe this is the reason why Queen Elizabeth levied special taxes on people with beards - and scores of noblemen suddenly appeared in her court with their beards shaved off and their whiskers colored with white powder.

Five hundred years ago, it was said that "the beard, in its full form, is a sign of the man's maturity and wisdom." This is why men nurtured their beards, and this is why in later eras shaving and a smooth face were considered "liberal" or revolutionary!

Bed

There are many superstitions linked to beds - mainly because of the fact that a person spends a large part of his life in it, and mainly because he usually dreams while he is in bed. The bed is a dangerous place, and it is a fact that many deaths occur when people are lying in bed.

A widespread superstition states that you must always get into or out of bed on the correct side. You must always remember that the left side is controlled by the devil. A remedy for this is putting on your right sock first every morning.

A powerful superstition is that the bed must never be made by more than two people, since the third (plus any other) person will always be in mortal danger.

It is possible to prevent bad luck or the evil eye from following the person to bed in two ways. One is not to walk in a straight line from the door to the bed, but rather to make at least two turns in the room, so that the bad luck loses its way. The other is to leave a dish of cold water under the bed to throw out of the window every morning.

Under no circumstances must a hat be placed on the bed!

After making the bed in the morning, many people are in the habit of peeking under the bed - not to look for their lover, but to deter the devil from approaching the bed.

Some people sprinkle salt or flour around the bed - also as protection against the devil (who is afraid of making footprints when he comes near the bed). Since this method involves cleaning the room every day, it is not recommended.

In the West, the bed should stand in a west-east direction. But the direction changes in many places, according to local beliefs concerning "energy flows.

Black cat

The black cat is a central figure in superstitions. It is difficult to find the origin of the superstition. In ancient Egypt, the cat was a sacred animal, and the black cat was considered to be the pet of the god of death. The belief was that when you treated the god of death's pet well, he was grateful to you in the world of the dead! In the Egyptian "Book of the Dead," we find many descriptions of jewels that were given to the black house cat. In many cases, the cat was killed and mummified so that it could be buried with its owner, in preparation for the resurrection of the dead.

In Europe, the black cat was considered to be the constant companion of the wicked witch. We find that the black cat was harnessed to Freija's sled - the wicked witch of the north. In this capacity, the black cat assumes the form of a black horse, and after seven years of pulling the sled, he is rewarded - by turning into a wicked witch! This is the source of the north European belief that a black horse is bewitched, and it is forbidden to stroke it.

In the Middle Ages in Europe, everything concerning ancient Egypt was considered "sorcery" or "black magic." This is why the black cat, the good omen, became a symbol of black magic. Witches were described with a black cat beside them, and the superstition claimed that the witch could turn into a black cat - and a black cat could turn into a witch as a reward for its services.

Therefore, when a black cat crosses your path, it could be an omen that you will encounter a wicked witch or demon.

A black cat is dangerous to infants and elderly people, especially during sleep. This is because the cat, in order to turn into a witch, must take the person's soul, and it does this by "stealing his breath." There are many pictures depicting the cat, sometimes in the form of a cat-woman, crawling on the person's chest and stealing the breath/soul.

However, a black cat also brings good luck. When a sailor goes off to sea, the black cat that stays at home guarantees that he will return home, and ensures that the sailor's wife remains faithful!

A well-known English play from the 18th century describes a sailor's wife who hides her black cat in the laundry basket before her lover arrives.

A tale... and a warning:

"If the cat in your house is black -
you will not have luck in love."

In many places, a black cat that visits the yard of the house is a good omen, but becomes a bad omen when the cat decides to make the yard its permanent home!

The attitude differs from place to place. In the United States and Latin countries, a black cat crossing your path is a bad omen, and some people turn back and take another route. In contrast, in Japan, this is a sign of good luck! In England, some people consider a black cat coming toward you to be a sign of good luck, while a black cat going away from you is a sign of bad luck.

Blacksmith

There are many superstitions concerning a blacksmith and his trade. It is important to understand that the blacksmith, by virtue of his involvement with metal, which changed man's life, was credited with a great mystical ability - he transformed metal and molded it.

A village that has a blacksmith is a "lucky" village, and is protected against visits by demons and ghosts. However, no faking is allowed in this matter: only when the smithy's furnace is hot (not necessarily when the fire is burning) does the blacksmith have protective powers.

The blacksmith has "natural healing" abilities, especially when it comes to children. Many of the early forms of healing involved burns, and a smithy was the most suitable place to find molten iron!

When a blacksmith's anvil cracks, it is a bad omen that foretells imminent disaster or death! In contrast, when the blacksmith's hammer breaks, there is nothing significant about it.

In many places, operating the bellows while the blacksmith is hammering horseshoes is considered to be an occupation that brings the person a great deal of good luck, and even cures diseases.

The water with which the blacksmith cools the molten metal is used as healing water in which to bathe the body.

However, committing adultery with a blacksmith, and especially with the blacksmith's apprentice, is liable to lead to the birth of a child who is physically or mentally handicapped!

Button

Buttons were very valuable ornaments on garments until the 14th century, when they were also used as fastenings. Before that, buttons had mainly been used as a very expensive decorative element, crafted by an artist from expensive materials. The accepted superstition has it that a button that is given as a gift is an extremely valuable amulet for the person.

Of course, if a "personal" button fell into the hands of a person's enemy it could be used for using black magic against him.

A button is also very useful in predicting the future. Let's say that a person wants to know who his future mate will be. All he has to do is write the names of possible candidates on a piece of paper, take a handful of buttons, and begin to place them on the names, from first to last (and back, if the number of candidates is small, or the number of buttons is large). The name that gets the last button is his intended!

It is important to remember that if the person buttons his clothes in the wrong buttonhole, he will have bad luck during the entire time he wears that item, even if he corrects the mistake.

Candle

The candle is a very important item in superstitions. Its main function is to bring light into places where human beings go, and to dispel the darkness, of course. Darkness is linked to the evil eye, and light to good luck. Therefore, the burning candle is a tried, tested, and accepted means of getting rid of the evil eye.

There are many superstitions linked to it. Some people light candles around a dead body (generally 12 candles) in order to create a ring of light.

Others light three candles (in parallel to the Holy Trinity) for the same purpose.

The candle, especially the candle that is found in holy places - churches or the graves of saints - is important for making potions and amulets. There is a great deal of belief in the power of a "holy" candle to help a barren woman to conceive, or to strengthen a man's virility, and there is no doubt about the link between the shape of the candle and of the male member.

A burning candle gives off light, and this light is very significant. Blue light emanating from the candle always attests to good luck, for instance.

When a candle goes out during a religious ritual, it is irrefutable proof that the evil eye is in the vicinity, and that the forces of evil are invading the candle's light!

Candles, which were made principally out of beeswax in the past, were thought to be holy because of the belief that bees originated in the Garden of Eden. This is the source of the belief that chewing the remains of holy candles fortifies health and contributes to the curing of serious illnesses.

Candles can serve as voodoo dolls when necessary. Sticking pins in the candle, while pronouncing the name of the person's sweetheart will strengthen the bond of love. The pin must be stuck in the candle, which is then lit and allowed to burn down. The scorched pins must be carried as an amulet of love.

Carrying a bride over the threshold

The custom of a man carrying his bride over the threshold of the house or of the bedroom is very widespread. The origin of this custom is ancient. In Europe, in poor communities, when there was no money for the couple to pay for a marriage license, the two would hold hands and jump over a broom. This was considered a legal marriage, and they could register as a married couple in the community or church registers.

This custom of jumping over a broom, in conjunction with the conquering male who hits the virginal woman on the head and drags her behind him in order to ravish her, led to the custom of carrying a bride into the house where she would be deflowered. The bride displays a cautious measure of restraint and reluctance, and the man demonstrates his virility and his strength in a civilized way.

It is a very bad omen for the bride to slip out of the man's arms before he gets her into the house. (Once inside the house, both of them can fall down!) In many cases, this tragic event can even cause the marriage to be annulled.

The fact that this custom was thought to be an essential ingredient for future happiness caused many contemporary feminists to oppose it... or to carry their husbands over the threshold!

Clock of death

There is a superstition that says that when a person dies in a house, one of the clocks in the house stops. If a person dies and a clock does not stop, the family should take a clock and shatter it in order to uphold the custom - otherwise death is liable to come back again!

In many places, it is customary to bury the shattered clock with the person.

Cupid (Eros)

Cupid is the Latin name for the Greek god of love, Eros. He is Venus' son by Mercury, and he symbolizes everything to do with passion, lust, and love - and all the attendant problems! Popular beliefs attribute a great deal of power to him in creating bonds of love between two people.

In general, he is described as a sweet youth, naked and winged. He is armed with a bow and arrows, and his arrows pierce his victims with love. When his arrow strikes the earth, a plant that augments love blooms, and is used in love potions.

Sometimes his eyes are covered so as to indicate that love is blind. This is the origin of the saying, "Love is blind."

Cupid and his image serve as "the amulet of love" and as a sign of love.

Dead but not dead

A common belief has it that when there is an erroneous announcement of a person's death, the "dead" person is granted another seven happy years of life. This is the origin of the custom, which is widespread in Central Europe, to publish death notices about a person when he is suffering from a serious disease! In this way, hopefully, Death will be confused, and the person will recover.

Dog

There are many superstitions linked to dogs, some of which are flattering to man's best friend, and some of which are not:

When dogs bark and play, it is a sign that a prophet (and in other version the Messiah, son of David) is in the vicinity.

When a dog howls like a jackal, it means that the angel of death is nearby.

In contrast, when a person leaves his house, and the first thing he sees is a friendly dog jumping around him and not baring its teeth at him at all - it is a sign that the person will have a perfectly good day. (Of course, the moment the person's back is turned, the dog is liable to bare its teeth!)

When a rabid dog bites a person, the person himself must kill the dog, otherwise he will die, heaven forbid.

If a person is afraid of dogs, he should carry the tooth of a black dog in his pocket - and then dogs will be calm when he is around. And if the person carries the (dried) heart of a black dog, he will be protected against dogs and acts of sorcery. As it is said in the sources, "and he can soak the heart in strong spirit [alcohol] of burned wine so that it will not decay quickly," since the heart of a black dog is quite rare.

Donkey, ass

The donkey is a most peculiar animal from the point of view of popular belief. On the one hand, the donkey is considered to be a stupid beast, good only for carrying loads, and on the other, properties concerning human wisdom are attributed to the she-ass, such as in the case of Balaam's she-ass.

When a donkey bends its ear on a sunny day, it is a sign that rain will fall before evening.

The donkey has a cross-like bone on its neck, and the superstition states that this bone is a sign of Jesus' ride to Jerusalem on a white donkey. This is the origin of the Christian belief that when a child is ill, it can be placed on a donkey and walked in a circle, and in this way the disease will pass.

When a donkey disappears, you should not try to find it, because the donkey knows when it is about to die, and it goes off on its own to die (this belief is true for elephants as well). As we know, we must not go looking for death!

For this reason, there is a saying, "It is impossible to find a dead donkey," and this reinforces the belief that when the corpse of a donkey is found, death is no longer in the vicinity.

The donkey is linked to adultery. In many cases, men who were caught in strange beds turned into donkeys in order to confuse the cuckolded husband. The origin of this belief lies in Apollonius' story, "The Golden Ass," which attributes great virility to the donkey.

Door

Doors are very significant in popular belief. The door is the entrance to the home, just as lips or eyes are the entrance to the person. Amulets against the evil eye are always placed on the front door, and generally only on that door.

An accepted belief states that when a baby is born in the house - or, heaven forbid, a person dies in the house - the door must be kept open to let the "carrier of souls" go to and from the body.

When there are several doors in the house, they must not all be open at the same time. It is especially important to ensure that when the front door is opened, the back door, if there is one, is properly closed. This superstition stems from the fear that an evil ghost, or the evil eye, will get into the house through an unprotected doorway.

In Rome, it was believed that when a person entered a house left foot first, he brought bad luck to the house and to its occupants! In the homes of the rich, a slave was responsible for letting strangers into the house, and his job was to ensure that they all placed their right foot on the threshold. Sometimes, a special step was placed at the entrance to the house with a surface for placing the right foot only.

There is a similar superstition in the East, where entering the house with shoes on brings bad luck. This is the origin of removing one's shoes before entering a house of prayer.

A house whose front door faces the street is a house that brings good luck to its occupants (and this is the origin of the difference in price between a house that faces a main street, and a house that faces an alleyway).

In Central Europe, in a house where someone has died,

it is forbidden to slam a door for three days. The noise is liable to anger the spirit of the dead person. A similar custom exists among many tribes in Africa and Asia - it is forbidden to sweep dirt out of the door for a year after a person has died in the house, for fear that it might harm the spirit.

Earring

From ancient times until this very day, earrings have been considered extremely valuable amulets. In China, for instance, the ear is thought to be a "miniature map" of the human body, and the location of the earring on the ear can determine the person's future.

It is interesting that women wear earrings for esthetic and ornamental reasons, while men wear an earring in one earlobe because of superstition.

The origin of this belief is similar to the origin of the custom to pull a child's ear - to cause him to develop his intelligence! The belief was that the ear was the "gate of wisdom," especially in the olden days when learning was done mainly aurally - and pulling on it "expanded the mind." The earring replaced ear-pulling. This is also the reason why men wore only one earring - so that there would be an opening on one side for wisdom to enter and no opening on the other side out of which the wisdom could escape!

Egg

There are many superstitions concerning eggs in general, and hens' eggs in particular.

An egg that is unusually small predicts an imminent death!

Every tenth egg laid by a hen is bigger than the nine previous ones, and is lucky for the person who eats it!

Eggs must not be gathered and brought into the house after midnight, because there is a danger that bad luck will sneak into the house together with the eggs.

An egg without a yolk brings bad luck, and superstition has it that it was laid by a rooster. In many cultures, it is forbidden to eat such an egg; the person who does so runs the risk of losing his children.

An egg with a double yolk is an omen of an approaching death.

When a hen sits on an odd number of eggs, bad luck will strike the house and its occupants.

Sailors at sea do not mention the egg by name, but speak instead about "balls." We could not find an explanation for this custom.

When eating a soft-boiled egg, it is forbidden to throw the eggshell into the fire. The shell should be crushed and buried in the earth. (Witches collect eggshells that haven't been crushed and use them to cast their evil spells in all directions!)

A young girl who wants to know who her beloved will be, or who her bridegroom will be, boils an egg until it is hard, extracts the yolk, pours a heaped teaspoon of salt onto the white, and eats the whole egg while she is alone in the room. She is sure to see the face of her future beloved in her dreams that night.

In Japan, it is forbidden for a woman to walk on an eggshell, because such an act immediately attests to the fact - as surely as a thousand witnesses - that she has lost her mind! This superstition is similar to the one that prohibits walking under a ladder.

Elbow

When the elbow itches, it means that very soon, the person will find himself sleeping in a strange bed. Some people expand on this and say that a partner of the opposite sex will also be keeping company in the same strange bed!

When a person gets a blow on the elbow, it is a bad sign that can only be deflected by striking the other elbow!

When a person wants to take revenge on someone who did him wrong, he bites his own elbow while imagining his enemy in front of him. He can rest assured that something bad will happen to his enemy. This, of course, requires quite a bit of flexibility on the part of the avenger.

Emerald

The emerald is reputed to have many properties:

Drinking nine grains of emerald powder with a glass of water, on an empty stomach, cures stings and poisonings.

An emerald hanging around a person's neck will strengthen his stomach and cure epilepsy.

An emerald held in the mouth will strengthen the teeth and the digestive tract.

An emerald placed in the anus will mend the intestinal tract and revive a person who has fainted.

And it is a law that whoever uses an emerald must only do so eight hours after eating.

Encounters with animals

When a person encounters an animal unexpectedly, it is an omen of the future. In fact, there is a whole theory about predicting the future according to chance encounters with different animals, which is called aphantomancy. This theory originated in periods in which man lived in closer proximity to nature, and such encounters were everyday occurrences.

When the person sees a bird of prey, such as an eagle or a buzzard, catching a snake in its beak or talons - this is a suitable place to build a house!

According to a Mexican legend, ancient Mexico City was built by the Aztecs in the place where the king saw a giant eagle grasp a snake in its beak and soar up into the blue skies.

There are animals with which an encounter is a sign of good luck: a ram, a hedgehog, a horse, a white mouse, a white rat, a sheep, a squirrel, and so on.

There are animals with which an encounter is a sign of bad luck: a bat, a wounded dog, a black or gray mouse, a fleeing hare, a black rat, or a wild boar.

Other animals are considered to bring good or bad luck according to the culture and the specific case: a black cat can foretell good or bad luck in different cultures. A snake crossing one's path can symbolize bad luck - or an abundance of good luck!

Cuckoos herald an abundance of good luck as long as they utter their call during the encounter. Birds such as doves, robins, wagtails, warblers, and swallows bring good luck. Crows, owls, hawks, or kingfishers are bad omens.

Among the insects, ants, bees, grasshoppers, crickets, and certain beetles (such as ladybirds) bring good luck, as long as there are at least three of them together. Wasps, spiders, and cockroaches bring bad luck, even when they are on their own.

In all cases, the person must see the animal, not just hear or feel it.

There are superstitions that are unique to a particular animal - such as a cat - or to a group of animals, such as horses, birds, or fish.

Whenever the superstition is significant, there is an explanation in this book.

Eternity

This is a well-known Chinese sign that signifies eternity through the meeting of rivers and the flow of water. The "drop" above it indicates the higher meaning of the sign. The sign teaches superior harmony, higher than on the face of the earth. It has become an accepted amulet in the West although many people do not understand its precise meaning.

Evil eye

The general belief in the power of the evil eye is the most widespread superstition of all. The evil eye is the cause of most diseases, deaths, and troubles in the world, and it is man's biggest enemy. This belief is common to every culture and place in the world.

There is a deeper belief here, a belief that an evil thought can have an actual physical effect on a person. For this reason, the person must always guard against the evil eye.

The connection with the eye is clear. In former times, the eye, the sense of sight, was the strongest link with one's surroundings. When a person was punished by having his eyes gouged out, it was more serious than capital punishment! Some people claim that the fact that the eye reflects the outside world also contributed to the importance of the eye.

It is obvious that the person's first concern is to protect himself against the evil eye, that is to defend himself against the negative influence that somebody can have on him. Many superstitions are inextricably linked to this belief in the evil eye.

This protection is not in the least easy. The devil is unbelievably cunning, and, sometimes the evil eye is disguised in a mask of a "blessing" or of goodness. For instance, when people say, "What a beautiful baby!", it is imperative to immediately protect the baby against the evil eye.

Protection against the evil eye takes many forms, among them: putting blue shadow beneath the eye, placing a mezuzah at the entrance of the house, or spitting noisily over the left shoulder so as to blind the devil!

The origin of many superstitions lies in the fear of the evil eye. We must remember, however, that the evil eye also serves as a valuable tool when we want to harm someone else (even though he is liable to use the defense of "sending it back to you," and then you're in trouble again!)

Eye shadow

Eye shadow, the color with which a circle is drawn around the eye, originated in ancient Egypt, where they would draw a circle, mainly in blue, around the eye. In this way, bad luck, or the evil eye, could not penetrate and harm the person. The devil and the forces of evil had no control or power over the barrier of this eye shadow.

Some people claim that blue eye shadow also has the power to cure eye diseases and to provide protection against eye maladies.

As is stated in an ancient Greek book about health, "People whose eyes have weakened should quickly to heal their eyes with Kohl...".

Fish

The fish is very significant in the superstitions of various cultures. Even in ancient cultures, fish was thought to be good for the brain, and an old saying states that if a person does not eat fish at least once a week, his intelligence becomes thinner than water.

In order for a fish to bring good luck, it must be eaten from head to tail, in that order.

If a fisherman counts the fish he has caught, he won't catch more fish that day.

The first fish that the fisherman catches in his net or with his rod must be thrown back into the water as a gift to Poseidon, god of the sea.

In many places in the world, the fish is considered to be a sacred creature that must not be eaten - and in some places it is claimed that the fish is the food of the spirits only.

The fish is linked to fertility rites. In ancient Egypt, it was believed that the fish is in fact the manifestation of the phallus of Osiris, and eating it increases fertility. In China, a man whose potency is weak is supposed to eat fish for seven consecutive days in order to regain his vigor. In Christianity, the fish is linked to the holy trinity (Jesus fed his followers with fish). In order to fulfill the commandment of rejoicing on the Sabbath as far as being fruitful and multiplying is concerned, fish must be eaten on Fridays; and so on. It must be remembered that a fish spawns thousands of young without any overt sexual activity - and for this reason is considered to have power and mystery in the realm of fertility and sexuality.

Four-leafed clover

A four-leafed clover - an extremely rare phenomenon, to the chagrin of believers - is used as a very lucky amulet, and the person who carries it in his pocket is sure to have wealth and happiness. And even more importantly - the four-leafed clover enables the person to see the occult, to invoke the spirits of the dead, and to communicate with fairies and angels!

The belief in the four-leafed clover is so extensive that an entire industry of fake four-leafed clovers has sprung up.

Frog

The frog (like the toad) has a place of honor among the superstitions, and not just in children's stories. The frog, like the fish that goes on dry land, is linked to fertility because of its numerous offspring.

A frog in the house means good luck for the house! This belief was widespread in Mediterranean countries. In ancient Egypt, it was customary to bury the dead with a "personal" frog. A frog sitting on a lovely maiden's lap promises that she will become pregnant before the first rain!

However, many superstitions link the frog to serious trouble. For instance, there is a superstition that frogs consume the souls of innocent babes. Another superstition has it that if a frog leaps in front of a man, it is a sign that his wife is cheating on him.

The use of a frog as an amulet is widespread mainly in South America, and has spread to the rest of the world. This amulet mainly appears in the form of medallions or embroidery on clothing and belts.

Different forms of the frog's body parts are used in potions for increasing fertility and virility.

Garlic

Garlic is generally linked to blood-sucking vampires. A chain of heads of garlic protects the person from vampires, especially during the night.

We must remember that garlic, by nature, is a disinfectant herb, and it was used over the generations as a prophylactic measure against diseases and epidemics. This health factor, together with the belief in the existence of vampires, led to a chain of heads of garlic becoming a matter of life or death in Europe. Today, too, many properties of good luck are attributed to garlic, in addition to properties of health.

A clove of garlic is effective against toothache, cures stomach-aches, restores the appetite (by smearing it on the gums), prevents bedwetting in children and urine incontinence in elderly people, and reinforces virility.

In ancient Greece, garlic was linked to Hecate, the goddess of death who was connected to sorcery and magic. After a meal, a clove of garlic is placed on the altar of Hecate. This is where the link between garlic and magic stems from.

The powerful odor of garlic has its own properties. Some people claim that the smell of garlic chases the devil away, while others claim that it attests to the proximity of the devil.

In ancient Rome, garlic was considered to give courage. The Roman soldiers would chew on cloves of garlic before going out to battle, and "the smell of their breath alone was enough to chase the enemy away," as one ancient historian noted. In other places in the world, fighters would smear mashed garlic over their bodies before battle. We find this custom to this day among the bullfighters of Mexico and Spain.

Getting out of bed on the right side

It is imperative for a man to get out of bed, or get into it, from the right-hand side only, otherwise he is risking his life. This superstition can often explain why there is "his" side of the bed and "her" side.

Although this is an ancient custom - known for about 500 years - we do not know its origin. Some people tended to link it to the manner in which noblemen's beds were placed - on the right-hand side of the bed there was a special pillar on which the man placed his sword or weapon.

Hand

From ancient times until this very day, the hand has been the focus of many superstitions. One of the most widespread superstitions in the world states that when the person's right hand itches, he will come into a lot of money, or he will get glad tidings! In contrast, if his left hand itches, he will soon suffer a financial loss. (In this case, the bad luck can be deflected by rubbing the left hand on a piece of wood, similar to the custom of "knocking on wood.")

When using a bowl of water to wash hands, two people must not use the same bowl, since this will lead to a quarrel between them. Thus, the water must be poured out and replaced by "fresh" water for the next person.

An old superstition says that it is forbidden to wash a baby's hands before its first birthday, otherwise it will not come into money when it grows up. In this case, the demands of hygiene clash with popular belief!

A damp hand attests to a sensual nature.

A cold hand means a warm heart.

A handshake with left hands is a bad omen. In many countries, it is considered indecent and insulting to offer one's left hand.

There are places where only the left hand is used for wiping and cleaning oneself after going to the bathroom, while the right hand is used for eating. Thus, holding out the left hand is considered a foul insult.

If a man and a woman shake hands, right hand with right hand, or left hand with left hand, and during the course of the handshake, their hands cross - it is the sign of an imminent wedding!

When a person sees his shadow on a night with a full moon, and his right hand is missing in the shadow, it is a bad omen that predicts the death of a male family member he loves!

When his left hand is missing in his shadow, it is an omen of the death of a female family member he loves!

(There is also a superstition that a finger missing in a shadow attests to the death of a close friend.)

Hat

For good luck, the brim of the hat must be turned so that the front part faces the back of the neck. In this position, the hat is supposed to protect its wearer from the evil eye and "turn" the state of things into good.

Another superstition concerning a hat is that wearing a hat under a roof brings bad luck. This is the origin of the custom of removing one's hat as soon as one enters a building.

Hiccups

Hiccups are a warning sign against the evil eye or against a person who is plotting evil against someone else. In order to get the evil away from the person, the hiccups must be stopped as quickly as possible! The practical side of the belief in hiccups is manifested in the different ways of stopping them. Some of them are:

Frightening the person - the person with the hiccups is frightened to the point of "his soul coming out"!

Drinking water - water is drunk in regular sips, the number of which corresponds with the person's age. This is particularly effective for people of 90 and above!

Bringing the thumbs very close together without them touching, and murmuring verses from the psalms or a prayer while doing so. Holding one's breath to the count of nine is another method.

In any event, the person must be careful of the evil eye until the hiccups stop, and keep a watchful and suspicious eye on everything going on around him.

Honeymoon

The concept of a honeymoon began with the custom of a newly married couple sipping a honey drink for the 30 days following the wedding. The drink was supposed to make the couple's life pleasant, to sweeten their mutual path, and to strengthen the man's virility and the woman's fertility. The 30 days comprise one cycle of the moon, and this means that in every cycle of life and its rewards, the sweetness will remain.

The honey drink was used in many cases to augment virility - without the wedding! Attila the Hun would mix honey with mare's milk and drink it before raping the women his warriors brought him on a daily basis. At least from that point of view, he spent his days in an eternal honeymoon.

At various times, the custom of the bridegroom "abducting" his bride and running away with her was widespread. The couple would hide away from their families for a month. Upon their return, they were considered married, with or without a wedding.

The prevailing belief to this day is that what begins during the honeymoon will continue throughout the couple's life.

Horseshoe

The horseshoe is a powerful amulet. The U-shape of the horseshoe is a powerful shape that protects the person against the evil eye and the dark forces. In most monotheistic cultures, this shape appears in the architecture of religious buildings and houses of prayer.

The origin of this shape lies, in fact, in the schematic representation of the female pubic region. Primitive tribes believed that the female pubis, being the essence of female power, had protective powers against the evil eye and the forces of the nether world. Ancient primitive art emphasizes the female pubis in various amulets not as a sexual object, but as a mystical amulet. Over the course of the generations, the horseshoe took the place of the female pubis.

The horseshoe is made of iron, and it is linked to the blacksmith - both the metal and the profession have powerful magical powers that provide the person with a shield.

An additional association of the horseshoe is with the horse - one of the domestic animals with the most significance for man, both at work and at war. Another association is with the crescent moon, a phenomenon with a magic spell of its own.

The typical horseshoe is fastened by seven sharp iron nails, and the number seven also has a great deal of significance as a number that protects the person. The horseshoe's seven nails, even without the horseshoe itself, can serve as an amulet - in the form of a ring reinforced by them - or as a "spice" for various potions in sorcery and magic.

In Greece and Rome, it was customary to nail a horseshoe to the doorframe as protection against the evil eye, and this custom spread all over the world. The power of a horseshoe found at the side of the road is particularly strong. According to the superstition, a demon that approaches the horseshoe will be "sucked up" into it. (This follows the link between the pubis and the horseshoe.) Another belief states that the horseshoe creates energy around it and chases the demon away.

Devils and demons try to seduce blacksmiths into nailing horseshoes onto their heels. (The devil has hooves like those of a horse, as we know.)

A well-known story tells of the Archbishop of Canterbury, who was a blacksmith's apprentice in his youth. One day, the devil came to the smithy, gave him a gold coin, and asked him to nail a horseshoe to his foot. The blacksmith's apprentice recognized the devil's wiles, and instead of nailing a horseshoe to his foot, he caught the devil and tortured him with molten iron until he promised never to set foot in a house with a horseshoe on its door. For this reason, the horseshoe is known as an amulet called "the sign of the Archbishop."

Today, the horseshoe is one of the most common amulets in the world, and we find horseshoe-shaped decorations on wedding cakes, in bouquets of flowers, on greeting cards, in cars, and so on. The shape of the horseshoe is very common in body paintings or tattoos.

According to the theories based on Freud and his followers, a horseshoe in a dream is quite important. The horseshoe is always an expression of the female pubis, parallel from this point of view to the snake that symbolizes the male member.

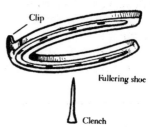

Clip

Fullering shoe

Clench

Itching

Itches in various parts of the body are omens of the future. This superstition occurs in various versions in all cultures. Among others, we find that when a young girl's nose itches, it is a sign that she will kiss a fool, or meet a charming stranger. If the left eye itches, it is a bad omen. If the right eye itches, it is a good omen. If the right palm of the hand itches, it is a sign of a lot of money coming the person's way. However, an itchy left palm indicates a loss of money If a virgin's heel itches, it means that she will soon be a bride.

Knife

The knife used to be a very expensive and personal item, so it was natural for many superstitions about it to spring up. The knife was also used for important things in the person's life - eating (cutting food), warfare, and work.

A knife, therefore, is one of the objects that protects against the evil eye and the devil. A knife stuck in the front door will protect the house against the evil eye. A knife stuck in the baby's crib will guard the baby from bad luck.

It must be remembered that the shape of a knife resembles that of a cross, so the knife is a very common amulet, especially in Christian countries.

When you see a devil or a witch, you must throw a knife at them to chase them away. Since they leave a whirlwind in their wake, it is preferable, for safety's sake, to throw the knife when you notice a whirlwind passing your house.

When a knife and fork are placed crossed on the table after a meal, it is a sign of an imminent quarrel!

Altogether, dangerous objects must not be crossed, since this act is reminiscent of the crucifixion itself (and not of the cross, which is considered an amulet).

When a knife falls on the floor, it is a sign of good luck.

When a knife falls and its blade gets stuck in the ground, it is a sign of an approaching guest.

When a knife falls and its blade does not get stuck in the ground, you can expect a row in the near future.

Don't sharpen a knife after dark. Doing so can generate serious financial or physical consequences!

Farmers believe that a knife must not be left on the table overnight. This will cause the death of one of the household pets the next day.

Because a knife is so sharp and dangerous, it must never be given as a free gift - that is, a gift for which you get nothing in return. Therefore, when a person receives a knife as a gift, he must immediately give the giver a small sum of money, or some other object - even something of minimal value. And it doesn't hurt to add the wish, "May our love [or friendship] stand firm forever, even against the sharp knife!"

Knock on wood!

This is an important superstition that must not be ignored. Touching or knocking on wood reinforces the possibility of a wish coming true, and gets rid of the evil eye. When we knock three times in quick succession, the effect is much greater.

The origin of the custom is unclear, but there are several possible explanations. One is that people used to live in trees for reasons of safety, and the custom of knocking on wood originated there. Another is that wood symbolizes the cross on which Jesus was crucified, and knocking on wood deflects bad luck because the sound is reminiscent of the nails being driven into the cross.

Knot

A knot is a very important way of guarding a person, and not just a way of remembering things. Examples of this can be seen in various phenomena in everyday life.

A knot is a way of capturing the devil and his henchmen, and whoever ties his necktie or his belt with a knot is liable to trap the devil in it! That is why a Christian priest's "dog-collar," for instance, has no knot, so that the devil will not get caught in the knot and be dragged by the priest, heaven forbid, into his church.

Women are in the habit of tying a big knot in their aprons when they work in the kitchen in order to protect themselves, because the kitchen or pantry tempts the devil.

If a knot is tied during a wedding, it can lead to the couple being childless! The only counter-remedy is to undo the knot before the end of the wedding.

In contrast, knots and fastenings on the bridal garments contribute to a long, ongoing marriage, and this phenomenon is common both in East and West. Not for nothing did one of the researchers claim that in the past the man devoted more time to untying all of the knots on the bride's clothes than he devotes to his entire marriage today!

The importance of nullifying the fate that is determined by a knot is illustrated in the story of the Gordian knot, cut by Alexander of Macedonia. Only the nullification, or untying, of the knot sets the man free to act in his own way, and to determine his fate by himself.

Ladder

Passing or walking under a ladder that is leaning against a wall brings bad luck - and not only when the ladder falls on you!

The origin of this superstition lies in ancient symbolism. The shape of the triangle or the pyramid expresses life. The ladder leaning against the wall creates this shape. The person who passes under the ladder damages and "desecrates" the symbol of life.

Another superstition states that the ghosts of the dead lurk under the ladder - especially those of criminals and sinners who did not get into paradise - and they trap victims. This superstition stems from the fact that in the past, the gallows resembled a ladder leaning against the wall.

What happens if you pass under a ladder without noticing it? The ill effects can be deflected, as follows:

Under the ladder, you must quickly make a wish. The wish will not come true, since it will be snatched away by the ghost - but you will come out unscathed!

You can cross your fingers, as if to say, "I'm not really going under a ladder."

You can retrace your steps without turning to look back, and bypass the ladder at a safe distance.

Sometimes we find the ladder to be a positive omen. In Egypt, it was believed that the ladder was used by the god Osiris to escape from the gloomy nether world. Jacob's ladder in his famous dream was used by the angels from heaven. Thus we find amulets in the form of ladders. It is certainly possible that the person who carries an amulet like this can pass under a ladder unharmed, but it is also possible that the ghost lying in wait for him isn't Egyptian, and doesn't know this particular Egyptian tradition.

Lightning

Lightning, like thunder, is a sign of the activities of God or the gods. We must remember that lighting and thunder are phenomena that man experiences from birth, without being able to explain them logically or even according to his understanding.

Many superstitions linked to lightning have been collected over the years:

Lightning does not strike twice in the same place.

When lightning strikes a person or an object, it is a sign that "his external appearance does not reflect what's inside him," or, in other words, that he is a bit of a fake.

An acorn provides effective protection against lightning.

Lightning is attracted to a dog's tail, especially a stupid dog. When lightning splits the sky, milk - even in a nursing mother's breasts - goes sour!

Lizard

A lizard inside the home is a sign of good luck for the home and its inhabitants. Under no circumstances must it be harmed!

Love at first sight

"Love comes through sight, and there is no love stronger than love at first sight," according to an old English saying.

According to the superstition, every person, man or woman, is half of a pair that was separated during "the descent to Earth"; this is why everyone searches for his or her "missing half" from the moment of birth. The missing half is identified at a glance - and that's love at first sight!

In various cultures, there are different cultural aids that lead to love at first sight, such as forbidding the groom to see his bride before the wedding, so that he will love her as his wife at first sight. In many cases, there is a description of sleep or darkness, and the moment the person opens his eyes, he sees his beloved before him. This is what happens in fairytales such as "Sleeping Beauty" or "Snow White" for instance.

In *A Midsummer Night's Dream*, Shakespeare mentions a flower that grew in the place where Cupid's arrow fell on the ground, and from which a potion was prepared that caused the person to fall in love with the first thing he saw upon opening his eyes. This potion is placed on the eyes of Bottom, asleep in the forest, who, upon waking, falls in love at first sight with... an ass!

Mirror, looking-glass

There are many superstitions connected with a mirror or looking-glass. It must be remembered that in the past, mirrors were not only made of glass, but also of polished metal (that is why a broken mirror was extremely significant).

A popular belief states that the mirror shows the person as he really is, without beating about the bush. "Mirror, mirror on the wall, who is the fairest of them all?" is a very common question. In the same way as a person can see himself, he can also see his intended mate in the mirror.

The mirror is closely connected to the prediction of the future and the occult - the crystal ball is, in fact, a kind of mirror.

In Iraq, there is a belief that when a person is ill, his mate should take a mirror that has been blessed by a holy man and look into it. If the mate sees the image of the sick person in it, it is a sign that he will recover completely.

Another belief claims that the devil or his henchmen always hide behind a mirror. This comes from the belief that the devil does not like to stand in front of a mirror (because he doesn't want to see himself in it), or that the devil, like a vampire, does not have a reflection in a mirror, and he is afraid that this fact will expose his true identity.

In Italy, for instance, women are in the habit of crossing themselves before they go to a mirror, not because they are afraid of what they will see, but for fear of the devil hiding behind it.

Breaking a mirror is an extremely bad omen. The person who breaks one lets himself in for seven years' bad luck! This superstition is common throughout the world. It originates from the days when the mirror was a very expensive item.

We must remember that the mirror in its natural form - that is, pools of water that reflect an image - was a tool of the gods. The gods revealed themselves to mortals, or sent signs to them, through reflections in pools of water (such as the reflection of the moon in a lake, for instance). Thus the mirror became a "holy vessel."

As we saw, breaking a mirror brings seven years' bad luck, since seven is the "mystical cycle" in which the soul is repaired. In order to shorten the seven-year cycle, there is only one remedy: to bury the fragments of the mirror in the earth. Only in this way can the bad luck be deflected!

Another superstition states that if a mirror is cracked, there will be a death in the house in which it was cracked within a year! The superstition stems from the opinion that the mirror cracks as a result of too much sorrow about the death that it sees in the future. This is God's way of warning about the danger. The way to avoid this bitter event is by making a sacrifice in front of the mirror. (The sacrifice takes the place of the "dead" person who is seen in the mirror.)

It is forbidden for a baby to look in a mirror during the first year of its life!

When a person dies, all the mirrors in the house must be covered, mainly so that his soul will not become "trapped" in a mirror, thus preventing him from entering paradise.

Another superstition states that all the mirrors in a house where a death has occurred must be covered, since the spirit of the dead person looks in the mirror and seeks additional souls for itself. Very religious Jews turn the mirror to face the wall, or place it in a closet.

A mirror that falls off the wall and breaks is a sign of an imminent death in the house! (Go and check that the mirrors are secure, please!)

Vampires, demons, and witches are not reflected in the mirror because they do not have a soul - and the soul is what is reflected in the mirror.

A mirror must be framed on all sides, otherwise there is an opening for the devil to get in and lurk there.

Mouse

A mouse is a bad omen, and maybe this is the source of the fear or loathing of mice (before Mickey Mouse was created). When a mouse gnaws at an article of clothing or furniture in the house, it is a sign of imminent death. When a mouse abandons a ship, it is a sign that the ship is about to sink.

The mouse is the creation of the devil. According to the superstition, the mouse was not among the animals that were chosen to be in Noah's ark, and was put there by the devil in order to gnaw holes in the ark. Another superstition states that the mouse was thrown from the sky by the devil in order to spy for him and his henchmen.

Navel

The navel is very important for eastern peoples. The belief in Muslim countries states that when the first person was created, the devil saw him and spat on him in disgust. The saliva began to burn his flesh, and omnipotent Allah made haste to pinch his flesh and get rid of the curse. In the place where Allah pinched, the navel was created.

This is why there is a belief that the exposed navel is the source of bodily lust. In order to conceal it, a precious stone is placed in women's navels, and a girdle is tied around men's bellies. An exposed navel is the first step to the devil's temptations.

Number 7

Entire books can be written about the superstitions concerning the number 7, which is a magical number linked to mysticism, and is considered a lucky number. Below we will present several of them.

The world was created in seven days, and the seventh day is considered a unique day in the process of the Creation. This is the origin of the belief that a woman's seventh child is an especially lucky child. When a seventh child has a seventh child - in other words, the luck becomes multi-generational - the child will be lucky and will have supernatural healing powers, and a highly developed ability to see the occult. In many places, this seventh child of a seventh child becomes a shaman.

When the person's date of birth is divisible by seven - without a remainder - this is a sign of enormous good fortune.

There is a superstition that the person's luck or fate runs in cycles of seven years, and every seventh year there is a change in luck. It seems that the stories of Joseph in Egypt with the seven fat cows and the seven lean cows affected this superstition.

A date that includes seven is a lucky date. Imagine how lucky a person who was born on the date 7.7.1777 or something like that was!

There are people who believe that the addition of the digit 7 to personal data improves their luck, and so they round off their weight or height to numbers such as 77 kilos or 1.77 meters. This is also the reason why many products have the number 7 in their names.

Number 13

The number 13 is very important, mainly because of the fact that there is no consensus as to its meaning among the various cultures. Some cultures consider 13 a lucky number, while others see it as bringing nothing but bad luck!

In ancient Egypt, there were 12 steps to Heaven, with the 13th being eternal life. This is why the number 13 is lucky. This is apparently the origin of the bar-mitzvah ceremony for 13-year-old boys in Judaism.

In other cultures, the number 13 is a sign of bad luck. There is no room number 13 in hotels, there is no 13th floor in skyscrapers, and of course it is forbidden to invite 13 people to a festive meal - probably because of the fact that there were 13 people at the Last Supper, during which Judas betrayed Jesus.

Onion

The onion, like garlic (both of them bulbous plants that are used in cooking and for flavoring), is considered to be effective against diseases. In any case of fever or inflammation, an onion should be cut in half, and one half placed on each side of the bed overnight.

Onion juice smeared over the scalp prevents hair loss.

An onion eaten raw fortifies courage and increases the warrior's power.

In ancient cultures, the onion had a magical value because of the spiral structure of its layers. This is why we find vows that are sworn while the person is holding an onion. This is also why the onion is a sign of loyalty and integrity.

Dreaming about an onion is a good omen.

In Europe, the weather is predicted according to onion skins.

The onion makes the eyes water, and the superstition states that a handkerchief soaked with "onion tears" can serve as an amulet against the evil eye.

Pearl

The pearl is a unique stone, since it is created in a living organism in the depths of the ocean. There are various superstitions linked to the pearl: it shines at night (like a cat's eye), and watches over people at sea. It warns of diseases and dangers by changing color. It foretells imminent death when it loses its unique luster.

There is a belief that pearls are actually frozen tears that return to us in the form of pearls (as Shakespeare states in *Richard III*).

Pearls have the power to revive human life. This belief stems from the northern myth about Baldor, who died. The tears of his mother, Friga, brought him back to life, and those tears fell into the water and turned into pearls.

In the East, pearls are connected to femininity, mainly because of the legend about the origin of pearls: When the moon is full, the oysters rise to the surface of the water and catch the "moon dew" that later turns into pearls. For that reason, we find that pearls are linked to love potions and femininity.

Cleopatra would grind large pearls into powder and drink the powder with wine. An Indian proverb says that "a woman with a pearl in her belly - her husband's love for her will never die."

In short, diamonds are a girl's best friends, but she appreciates pearls, too!

Pepper

Pepper - black in most cases, but also red in certain cultures, especially Eastern ones - is a spice to which many superstitions are attributed. In Greece and Rome, pepper was considered a status symbol because it was so expensive. During the Middle Ages, pepper was used as a disinfectant spice, as an antidote to many poisons, and as an agent that enhanced women's fertility and health in "women's medicine."

When pepper - ground or whole - is spilled, it is a bad sign, similar to spilled salt, but much less so. It is possible to avoid the evil omen by throwing pepper over your left shoulder (the devil stalks people from behind on the left, and the angels guard them on their right; the pepper is supposed to blind the devil and prevent him from doing evil deeds).

In general, spilled pepper foretells an imminent quarrel between a couple or between friends.

Another superstition states that if you want an unwanted guest to leave your house - place a pinch of pepper under his chair!

If a person - especially a woman during menstruation - is suffering from an inflammation or a fever, he must not eat pepper.

An old saying states that he who has a sack of pepper in his cellar does not need gold bars in his home. This saying is based on the fact that in the past, pepper was "worth its weight in gold."

Pregnancy

In order for a woman to become pregnant, a rabbit skin must be burned to ashes, and given to her mixed in a glass of wine first thing in the morning. Nine days later, the woman will get pregnant as soon as she has intercourse with her husband.

Some people say that a fox skin is good for the same purpose, especially a red fox.

A barren woman must take the wax from holy candles, form half a ball, place seven drops of her menstrual blood in it, and then close the ball. Then she goes out alone at midnight and buries the ball of wax among the roots of a fruit tree. Seven weeks later, she will become pregnant, and the fruit tree will wither and never bear fruit again.

If a woman wants to become pregnant, she must not carry or wear anything made out of silver, since silver prevents pregnancy.

If a woman wants to become pregnant, and does not succeed in doing so, despite the fact that both she and her husband are sound and healthy, she should use this tried and tested method. She must take a pair of pigeons - male and female - slaughter them, and extract their brains while they are still warm. Then the woman must go and bathe, and when she has done that, she should sit on her bed, insert the pigeon brains into her cervix, and press on her vaginal opening with her left foot for a whole hour. At that point, she should have intercourse with her husband, and she will become pregnant immediately.

Pregnancy - boy or girl?

In order to know whether the woman is carrying a boy or a girl, she must urinate into a wooden bowl and stand a thick needle in the bowl for a day. Afterwards, she looks to see whether the curds from the urine surround the needle, like a pillar - and if so, she knows that she is carrying a boy. If the curds have sunk to the bottom of the bowl, she is carrying a girl.

Another method of knowing the gender of the fetus is by placing some of her milk in a dish of water in the ninth month. If the milk sinks, it is a boy. If it floats, it is a girl.

Yet another method of determining the gender of the fetus is to sprinkle a bit of salt on the woman's head without her being aware of it. Then start talking to her. If she begins to speak about a boy, then she is carrying a boy. If she speaks about a girl, it is a girl.

An additional method of knowing the gender of the fetus is by saying to the woman suddenly, "Show me your hands." If she shows you the back of her hands, it is a boy. If she shows you the palms, it is a girl.

Pyramid

The pyramid, known to us principally from ancient Egypt, appears in many beliefs - both because of its complicated and powerful structure, and because the pyramid is one of the most stable structures that man can build.

A pyramid made from three iron nails often served as an amulet at the entrance to the house, similar to a horseshoe.

The pyramid structure is thought to nourish body and soul, and fortify fertility and virility. That is why many people sleep under a pyramid-shaped canopy, or build a pyramid-shaped room in their home.

There is a belief that food that is placed in a pyramid never goes off.

Rabbit's foot

The rabbit's foot is very important in the field of sexual beliefs - and its influence is so great that it serves as a general good luck amulet. However, we will focus on a male rabbit's foot as a sexual amulet. Already in ancient times there was a belief that wearing or eating certain body parts transferred the properties of the eaten creature to the eater. A man who wanted to strengthen his virility would eat stallion testicles and rhinoceros horns - anything to become more potent.

The male rabbit, which was known mainly in Europe, was famous for its tremendous potency and its ability to copulate numerous times, and because of this, carrying a rabbit's foot transferred that same sexual property to the bearer.

In many places, it was customary to give youths a bow and arrow or a rifle and send them to hunt a rabbit and cut off its foot as the "initiation ceremony" that introduced them into the world of men.

Most importantly, a rabbit's foot must be carried in the left pants pocket - and we don't have the faintest idea why!

Razor, shaver

Razors or shavers are personal appliances, and the prevailing superstition states that they are personal objects that must not be used by anyone else, especially not a friend. A razor that is transferred to a friend is liable to "sever" the friendship.

Another superstition says that finding a razor or a shaver - and in certain places, a razor blade as well - is a bad omen, predicting that the finder will suffer a disappointment in the near future.

Salt

Amazing properties and superstitions have been attributed to salt since time immemorial. Salt is a crystalline substance that is produced as if by magic in water, and disappears in water. Salt is a pure product - that is, it does not contain any additional substances - that is white in color, and for this reason is considered to be "sacred." We must remember that in days of yore, salt was extremely valuable, expensive, and indispensable to human life. Salt was so expensive that in many countries, gathering and mining salt was the monopoly of the king or ruler.

Salt has good and bad properties.

The first superstition states that salt protects the person against the devil. This is why, when salt is spilled, it is a sign that the devil is in the vicinity, and the person's guardian angel caused him to spill the salt. Since the guardian angel is stationed behind the person's right shoulder, and the devil is behind his left shoulder, he must immediately take a pinch of the salt and throw it over his left shoulder in order to blind the devil!

However, spilled salt also foretells an imminent quarrel between a couple, perhaps as a result of the fact that in the past, salt was very expensive. "A quarrel with a husband always starts with spilled salt!"

Spilled salt is not only the sign of a quarrel, but also foretells days of sadness. In North America, it is believed that salt predicts sadness, since many tears are needed to "rinse out" the salt. For this reason, it is customary to pour salt onto fire, or onto a range - in order to "dry up" the tears of sadness. Obviously, the fact that tears are salty is connected to this superstition.

When salt is sprinkled on the threshold of the home, the devil and his henchmen cannot get in. (In fact, when salt or ash is sprinkled on the floor, the devil won't come because he is afraid of leaving tracks.)

In order to greet an important or beloved guest, the person must receive him with a gift in the form of bread and salt, or by placing a pinch of salt in his right hand.

If a pinch of salt is placed on a baby's tongue, he will have a long, happy, and healthy life.

Incidentally, salt was used as currency in the past, both in trade, and especially as soldiers' salaries. In fact, the word "salary" comes from "sal", the Latin word for "salt." This is where the saying, "he is not worth his salt," comes from.

There is a belief that salt provides immunity against poisons. This belief stems from the custom of former rulers, who would take a pinch of poison with their food in order to fortify their immunity against genuine poisoning. They mixed the poison with salt. This is the origin of the expression, "A pinch of salt a day prevents a change of ruler."

The expression, "salt of the earth," describes the cream of humanity. A Muslim proverb states that "salt was spilled between us," meaning that a covenant was sworn between people. In the East, salt is still a purifying and sanctifying substance. Salt is sprinkled in the Sumo wrestling ring before every match in order to purify it of the evil eye.

In Christianity, there is a belief that a person who spills salt is treacherous. Judas Iscariot, the man who betrayed Jesus and turned him in, is described as sitting at the Last Supper with a mound of salt on the table before him.

Scissors

When a woman drops a pair of scissors on the floor, she should ask another member of the household to pick them up, and not do it herself - not because of a backache, but because if the person who dropped the scissors picks them up, bad luck will follow!

If there is no one to pick up the scissors for her, she must stamp on the scissors with her right foot, and only then pick them up.

Some people go even further, claiming that when the scissors are back in her hands, she must rub them with her hands until she feels that the metal is warm, and only then resume using them.

Scissors are made of a metal that has great magical power, and a general belief states that anything sharp can "cut" luck. In this aspect, there is a similarity between scissors and a knife.

When scissors fall and stick in the ground, this is a bad omen that foretells a death in the near future!

When scissors break, the person can expect a bitter disappointment in the near future, especially in the domestic realm.

When a person gives someone else a pair of scissors, he should also give a silver coin along with the scissors, in order to neutralize the bad luck associated with them. When scissors are used for preparing a shroud or burial robe for a dead person, they must not be used for anything else, and should preferably be buried deep in the ground.

And finally - if you want to deprive a bride of her husband's virility, smuggle a pair of scissors into the church, and continuously open and close the scissors during the ceremony. This is a proven formula for taking away the groom's potency!

Shadow

There is a very common superstition that the shadow is an inseparable part of the person. When someone steps on another person's shadow, he brings bad luck to the owner of the shadow. When a person steps on his own shadow, he brings real misfortune on himself.

Another superstition states that when a stone falls onto the person's shadow, the person is in mortal danger. Sometimes a stone falling on a person's shadow is interpreted as a warning issued by the person's soul, warning the body of the threat of danger.

When the person is sitting beside a bonfire or a fireplace in which a fire is burning, and the shadow he casts looks as if it is headless - the person will die within a year!

When a man wants to conquer the heart and body of a girl who does not respond to his advances, he must stand next to her in such a way that his shadow falls on hers, and then she has no choice but to yield to his wooing.

Shark

The shark is an omen that frequently appears in the superstitions of sailors and maritime peoples. In the South Sea Islands, for instance, there are tribes who observe the behavior of sharks in the ocean, and interpret it as if it were a horoscope.

Sailors believe that sharks that escort the ship - especially a school of three or five sharks - foretell the death of one of the crew. The superstitions states that the shark can "smell" imminent death, and it follows the ship, waiting for the corpses to be thrown into the water.

This belief largely resembles that of birds of prey that circle a lone traveler in the desert, waiting for him to die.

Another superstition linked to sharks says that its organs, especially the fin that turns into its male member, can restore men's virility.

Shooting star

When you see a shooting star and make a wish, your wish will definitely come true!

When a star falls, it is a sign that someone has died (the star's path shows the soul the way to Heaven).

We must not point at a shooting star - or at any star - with our finger because we are liable to hurt the souls that are on their way up, or the angels that are guarding them.

There is a belief that while storks bring babies, shooting stars bring the babies' souls.

Stars in general are omens of good luck - and are therefore widely used as official symbols.

Snake

In every known culture, there are many superstitions linked to the snake - and we mean the actual snake, not the symbol of the snake in dreams or signs.

The belief in Judaism states that "he who carries a snake's head in his belt cannot be harmed by any man," and this could explain the many belt buckles that resemble snakes' heads! If a snake bit a person, the person had to rush to the nearest pool of water and drink from it - before the snake got there. A more modern superstition claims that it is preferable to rush to the nearest hospital!

The snake is linked to passion, or to lecherous acts - similar to the eel, which many people feel is even worse than the snake itself. There is a superstition that claims that poisonous snakes emerge from the body of a lecher after his death.

Perhaps that is linked to the superstition that in order to flee from a snake bite, the person must strip off his clothes and stand naked in front of the snake! Because of its modesty, the snake will turn around and disappear. Perhaps there is a distant echo of the Garden of Eden in this belief.

Another superstition has it that the snake has hypnotic powers in its glance, so it is forbidden to look directly into its eyes!

Sneezing

A sneeze, especially a noisy sneeze, is thought to be a "little death" in many cultures, or a state in which the soul is about to depart from the body. What is the remedy? The person must hear "Bless you," "God bless you," "Gesundheid," or some such blessing in order to set the soul right and prevent it from fleeing the body.

In many myths it is told that the world was created from God's "sneeze" - but when a person sneezes, he does not create a world, but rather causes the demons to come up to the surface. The blessing chases the demons back into the depths of the underworld.

A widespread belief states that anyone who sneezes three times consecutively will have eternal good health!

Spider

The spider frequently appears in myths and legends, especially when its web saves the good guy from the bad guys (King David in Judaism, Jesus in Christianity, and so on). For this reason, it is forbidden to disturb a spider, and under no circumstances must its web be destroyed.

There are many other superstitions linked to the spider: a mixture of crushed spider and honey cures fevers; tearing spider-webs is a sign that you will meet a friend; a female spider carrying the sac of eggs on her back indicates material abundance.

Spitting

When you feel the devil near you, spitting on the ground will chase him away.

When you are gripped by panic during the night, spitting loudly three times will get rid of the panic.

Before a competition, fight, or signing of a contract, you must spit on your hand (and preferably shake your opponent's hand while you're about it!)

Before getting into a ship or boat, you should spit on it.

A mother who fears that her child is in the grips of the evil eye must rush to spit on his head in order to dispel the danger!

A gambler who does not spit on his hand before gambling will come home with empty pockets.

When the devil is following you, spitting over your left shoulder will blind him, and he will lose you.

Among many tribes in Africa, spitting was considered to be a greeting of peace or of a safe journey. Saliva is an important ingredient in every healing drug that is made of earth or ash.

It is important to remember that spit is produced by the human body, and that saliva is "unique" to a particular person. Everything that comes from the body is very important in the field of superstitions concerning the evil eye.

An ancient superstition says that spitting is effective against snakes or poisonous insects. "Spitting on a snake will chase it away as if boiling water had been poured onto it. The purpose of saliva is to neutralize the snake's venom." Thus wrote Pliny, the Roman. This is perhaps why it is possible to heal a snake bite (according to the superstition) by licking or sucking out the venom. Don't try this! There isn't a single doctor who would recommend this method.

In natural medicine and healing, spitting is very effective. The Chinese believe that spitting gets rid of waste and the "seeds" of a disease, and this is why every self-respecting Chinese person spits ceaselessly.

Storms and tempests

Ancient tradition offers many signs according to which it is possible to know when a storm with wind, lightning, and rain will come. Among others:

If the sun rises out of a sea of fire, it is a sign that a tempest will arrive from the west.

If the stars twinkle like daisies in the night sky, but in part of the sky their eyes seem to close, a storm will come from that direction. A moon with a light ring around it foretells a wind from the sea.

When a strong wind blows, and suddenly dies down, it is a sign that within a short time it will become strong and turn into a storm that uproots trees and sinks ships in the heart of the ocean.

When schools of fish leap above the surface of the water, it is a sign that a heavy storm will come from the north. When there is a fog, and light is seen in it, it is a sign that a storm is on the way.

When animals such as turtles, fish, and birds are seen on the shore, and they are calm - it is the sign of a storm.

White foam on the surface of the water, without wind or waves, is a sign of the wind that will be coming from the sea. A golden wreath around a cloud predicts a rainstorm.

When a wind changes direction, it is the sign of an approaching storm. When the clouds are tinged with red an hour after sunset, it is a sign of a strong north wind.

An egg-shaped black cloud is a sign of an extremely severe storm.

Light on the surface of the water when neither the sun nor the moon is in the sky is a sign that one must prepare for a gale.

If the cock crows before first light - strong rain will fall before daybreak.

Tossing a coin

Tossing a coin to allow fate to help you choose between two options stems from the belief that a superior power intervenes and determines the person's path, and this intervention is expressed in the way the coin falls. The coin always has two sides, one of which is "heads" and the other "tails."

In Europe mainly, the expression "heads or tails" means "good luck or bad luck." This belief derives from the fact that in Rome, the emperor's portrait appeared on the coin - "heads" - and the other side was considered "tails."

In the days of Julius Caesar, the expression "the triumph of the emperor" was current: the emperor always conquers. Therefore, gambling on "heads" when tossing a coin was always for victory, while gambling against "heads" could be interpreted as treason against the emperor!

Trimming fingernails

Fingernails, or more precisely, fingernail parings, have a special place in popular beliefs. The fingernail is a part of the person, and according to superstition, control over a fingernail paring can give a magician or sorcerer the power to control the person himself.

When we want to put a curse on somebody, we look for one of his fingernail parings to use. This is why it is customary to burn or bury fingernail parings.

Another belief is that fingernails must be trimmed on appropriate days:

On Saturday (In Judaism, it is Saturday, In Christianity, it is Sunday; in Islam, it is Friday.), the paring is liable to fall into the hands of the devil, and then the person will also fall into his hands.

On Sunday, trimming the fingernails will cause your beloved to distance him/herself from you.

On Monday, trimming the fingernails will bring good news.

On Tuesday, trimming the fingernails foretells a shopping expedition.

On Wednesday, trimming the fingernails foretells a long journey.

On Thursday, trimming the fingernails foretells wealth.

On Friday, trimming the fingernails is a sign of a lot of money - and of terrible toothache!

As we said before, the big danger in trimming fingernails is that the parings - which are part of the person's body that of necessity contains part of his soul - will fall into the hands of the forces of evil.

Fingernails must not be trimmed according to the order of the fingers - this is dicing with death! In order to confuse the angel of death, you must skip from one finger to another randomly.

In many places, a long fingernail is considered to be an amulet for the person. First, it attests that the person did not "let go of" a part of his body, and therefore the forces of evil can't attack him. Second, it indicates that the person does not engage in manual labor.

It is possible to find many jewels in the shape of a thimble whose purpose is to protect the nail and to enable it to grow.

In noble families - especially the women - long, untrimmed nails are a clear sign of nobility.

White spots on the nails are very significant. The superstition states that a white spot on the nail causes the person to waste money - and a white spot on the thumbnail leads to great financial profit. The process begins the moment the piece of nail on which the spot appears is trimmed.

Other superstitions claim that a white spot on a nail is a sign of good luck; a white spot on the thumbnail means that the person will receive gifts or bequests; a white spot on the fingernail of the pinkie indicates a long journey; a white spot on the fourth finger foretells exciting news; a white spot on the index finger attests to friends; a white spot on the middle finger indicates enemies. As we said - the process begins when this part of the nail is trimmed.

Another superstition states that every lie told by the person manifests itself in a white spot on his fingernails, and maybe that's why there are people who trim their nails every day, for fear of the spots being discovered!

This also leads to the belief that chewing fingernails attests to a person's conscience not being clear.

Twin fruit

The meaning of twin fruit is two fruits of the same type that are joined together - for instance, two bananas in one shared skin. The superstition states that finding such a fruit is extremely lucky, and dividing it up between a couple, or between two friends, creates a very good atmosphere between them.

A pregnant woman who eats twin fruit may give birth to twins.

When a man eats twin fruit without sharing it with anyone, it is a sign that his life is controlled by two women!

Unicorn

The unicorn is a mysterious creature that features in almost every known culture. According to the belief, the unicorn disappeared from the world after it was expelled from Noah's ark. But can anyone say for sure where a unicorn that has not yet become extinct will suddenly pop up?

The unicorn resembles a horse, but what makes it special is the single, straight horn in the center of its forehead. Properties of purity and sanctity are attributed to the unicorn, and it symbolizes virginity, fidelity, and "human" warmth.

Only a virgin can touch a unicorn, and this is why the sign of the Zodiac for Virgo often depicts a young girl beside a unicorn, so that everyone will understand that she is a virgin. A piece of jewelry in the shape of a unicorn can symbolize the same thing.

The unicorn's horn, which is white, black, and red, can warn of danger, purify tainted water, and cure illnesses - all this just by a mere touch. Powdered unicorn's horn is an important ingredient in any magic potion, and it is especially effective for preparing a potion that makes the person invisible.

A pinch of powdered unicorn's horn restores men's virility, and is considered to be the ultimate aphrodisiac - and this is the reason why the rhinoceros, for instance, is becoming extinct. Its single horn is a substitute for the unicorn's horn!

Wedding anniversaries

Wedding anniversaries are considered to be very important dates, and the longer a couple is married, the more important the anniversary becomes. In order to safeguard the relationship for a long time, the couple must exchange gifts that are appropriate to the anniversary:

On the first anniversary, the gift is made of paper (such as a book).

On the second anniversary, the gift is made of cotton (an article of clothing).

The third - leather.

The fourth - flowers or embroidery.

The fifth - wood.

The sixth - sweets or an iron object.

The seventh - wool or copper.

The eighth - bronze.

The ninth - porcelain.

The tenth - tin.

The eleventh - steel (cutlery or a pot).

The twelfth - silk or fine fabric.

The thirteenth - delicate lace.

The fourteenth - ivory.

The fifteenth - crystal or fine glass.

The twentieth - delicate Chinese porcelain.

The twenty-fifth - silver.

The thirtieth - pearls.

The thirty-fifth - coral in the form of jewelry or a figurine.

The fortieth - a red stone.

The fiftieth - a gold object.

The fifty-fifth or sixtieth - an emerald.

And if you manage to reach your seventy-fifth anniversary, only a diamond will do!

Whistling

Whistling is very significant in the realm of superstitions, mainly because whistling is a way of communicating with or summoning the devil or his messengers.

Whistling in the home invites the devil into the home.

A little girl or a young girl must not whistle, as this will cause her to grow a beard!

It is forbidden to whistle on a ship or boat, and even more so to whistle at night. The belief is that Poseidon, god of the sea, thinks that someone is whistling at his wife, and his rage causes the sea to become turbulent. In contrast, it is permissible to whistle when the ship is tied to the pier, or is leaving port.

Whistling backstage in a theater causes the play to flop.

A miner who whistles underground can expect a landslide. This belief is similar to that of mountaineers who believe that a shout will cause an avalanche of rocks or snow.

A man who cannot whistle, according to the belief, has homosexual tendencies.

In Christianity there is a belief that when a woman whistles, she stimulates the pain of the Holy Virgin.

In ancient cultures, people feared whistling at night. It was believed that the person who whistled in the dark was inviting the devil. According to superstition, the devil awaits every sound that he can interpret as a call to him, and even the whistling of the wind in the branches of the trees is enough to summon him.

Wishbone

The wishbone is a bone in the chicken's breast, in the shape of a V, with a thicker apex. When two people each hold one end of the bone and pull, the bone breaks, and the apex remains on one part of it. The person who is holding the piece with the apex can make a wish that will undoubtedly come true.

This is an ancient custom, evidence of which we can find among the Greeks, the Romans, and the Etruscans. The rooster had prophetic and predictive powers attributed to it, since its crowing heralds the dawn. The hen lays an egg, which is a very well-known mystical shape. For this reason, chickens are wreathed in superstition.

When we want to predict the future using a rooster, we draw a magic circle, or a mystical circle of letters, and scatter grains over it. The rooster pecks at the grains, and its peck-marks are the signs of the prophecy. (This is similar to the circle of letters upon which the glass moves during a seance, for instance.)

A young girl can find a clue as to the name of her intended bridegroom in this way, when she sees where the rooster pecks at first. Moreover, if the rooster is slaughtered after the prophecy, its dried and crushed coxcomb can be used as a love potion!

Similarly, it is possible to predict the future or make a wish by pulling on a wishbone. When a person does this alone, he makes a wish and pulls on the bone. If the apex remains in his left hand, his wish will come true. If two people pull on the bone, the one who gets the apex will have his wish come true.

This custom is common all over Europe thanks to the Roman soldiers, who loved pulling wishbones.

When the bone breaks, the larger part is always the winning part. This is where the saying "Big is better than little" comes from, meaning that the big part always predicts the wish coming true.

Witch's dog

Everyone knows about the superstitions about a cat or a bat's link to sorcery. What is less well known is the superstition about the link between dogs and witches. In many places, especially in Central Europe, it is the dog that is thought to be the witch's companion, not the cat. This is probably a throwback to the image of the wolf, the ally of the forces of darkness. Some people claim that this belief comes from the fact that the dog is convenient to domesticate and train - and this property of training animals would seem to be an appropriate one for witches with a great deal of magical power.

However, it turns out that the origin of this belief is entirely different, and because of reasons of modesty and shame it is not discussed. In many places we find that women raised dogs for purposes of sexual intercourse. The first indication of this comes from Jewish sources, where we find a warning to the widow not to keep a dog in her house, so that it should not walk behind her in the market and cause people to gossip about her actions! In many trials of witches that were ostensibly conducted by the Christian church, the accusation "fornicated with a dog" appears.

In many places, we find a belief that a woman who lives alone may not have a dog in her house for fear of slander, but on the other hand, a dog in the house is very helpful in keeping various kinds of intruders at bay!

Yawning

Yawning is dangerous because it creates an opening through which the devil can enter the person's body, and for this reason it is imperative to cover one's mouth with one's hand while yawning!

In the olden days, it was believed that the yawn was an "inner" warning sign, warning the person of danger that was lurking in his path.

In India, a person who yawns snaps his fingers quickly three times in order to deflect the bad luck.

An actor who sees more yawns than applause in the audience should go and find another profession!